THE DIVINERS

THE DIVINERS

A POEM BY ~~ROBERT McDOWELL~~

Robert McDowell

PETERLOO POETS

1995

Published by Peterloo Poets:
2 Kelly Gardens, Calstock, Cornwall PL18 9SA, United Kingdom

Distributed in U.S. by Taylor Publishing Co., 1-800-677-2800; and Story Line Press, Three Oaks Farm, Brownsville, OR 97327-9718

The five chapters of this book, in earlier versions, have appeared in the following magazines: *Crosscurrents, The Hudson Review, Poetry Australia,* and *Pulpsmith.*

The first chapter, which originally appeared in *The Hudson Review,* was reprinted in *The Best American Poetry 1989,* edited by Donald Hall and David Lehman.

The author wishes to thank these publications, as well as Alfred Dorn, Dana Gioia, Mark Jarman, Beth Joselow, Frederick Morgan, Liam Rector, and Louis Simpson for their valuable suggestions and encouragement.

This book is for Lysa, Dylan, and Eoghan

and for

Barbara McDowell Campbell

Chapters

INTRODUCTION
by Dana Gioia

One of the most interesting things happening in American literature at present is the revival of narrative poetry. This broadscale movement, which cuts across several schools of poetry, attempts to regain some of the imaginative ground that eighty years ago Modernist verse ceded to prose. There have been a few genuine successes—Sydney Lea's "The Feud" and Charles Martin's "Passages from Friday," for instance—but generally this new direction in poetry has been more notable for its experiments than its unqualified achievements. It is no easy thing to reinvent a forsaken poetic mode.

The central difficulty of writing the new narrative poetry is easy to summarize—how does one create a compelling and credible story in verse without becoming prosaic? Modernism may be exhausted as a vital literary movement, but it permanently changed the contemporary sensibility. The transformation of poetic taste is nowhere more evident than in the almost impossibly high expectations now placed on narrative poetry. The evocative compression and lyric integrity of Modernist poetry left most readers impatient with the loose, expansive style of traditional narrative verse. The new narrative must tell a memorable story in language that constantly delivers a lyric *frisson*.

Contemporary narrative poets not only have the challenge of creating lyric stories; they must also invent cogent forms and intrinsically heightened styles in which to tell them. But what are those forms and styles? Modernism had so completely repudiated the narrative mode that by 1970 there was no available tradition. Young writers had to explore the past for useful precedents—not styles but starting points. Three neglected American masters provided the best examples—Edwin Arlington Robinson, Robert Frost, and Robinson Jeffers. Of these sources Robinson was probably the least immediately useful. His influence may momentarily surface in a poet like Jared Carter or R. S. Gwynn, but his importance has been mainly to reinforce the general virtues of compression, irony, and indirection in verse storytelling. Jeffers's legacy has been equally problematic. His tragic themes and sublime manner are not easily adapted by other writers. With the exception of Mark Jarman's extraordinary *hommage*, the book-length *IRIS* (1992), Jeffers's influence has also been mostly general. His work reminds contemporary poets how much the narrative mode gains from deep psychology, mythic subtext, and philosophical seriousness.

The quieter example of Frost, however, proved more widely useful. Frost's radical reinvention of the mid-length narrative poem in *North of Boston* (1914), *Mountain Interval* (1916), and *New Hampshire* (1923) may have gone unexploited by mid-century poets and mostly unnoticed by subsequent critics, but it suggested the most compelling possibilities for the contemporary poetic narrative—dark and passionate human stories told elliptically in evocative but understated language. Over the past decade he has emerged as the dominant influence on the New Narrative. Contemporary poets as dissimilar as David Mason, Julia Alvarez, Sydney Lea, Mary Jo Salter, Jared Carter and Robert McDowell have all been strongly influenced—though not restrained—by Frostian models. He has been a common departure point, though rarely a common destination.

Among these New Narrative poems, Robert McDowell's *The Diviners* is notable for its stylistic assurance and structural originality.

Whatever influences it bears from Robinson, Frost, and Jeffers—and McDowell has scrupulously studied all three masters—have been completely assimilated into a forceful style unlike any other contemporary book-length poem. By making the sharp transitions between episodes both an expressive device and the means by which he establishes an overall narrative rhythm, McDowell has boldly reinvented the structural dynamics of the long poem. He has not repeated the habitual Modernist mistake of recasting narrative material in a lyric mode and thereby preventing the larger work from building narrative energy. Instead, learning from the miscalculations of the Modernist epic (which even in the masterful hands of Pound, Crane, H. D., and Williams, could not satisfactorily cohere), McDowell has developed ways to compress the action—not only by compressing narrative description within each episode, but by eliminating the prosaic material of transitions. There is something essentially poetic about the way McDowell pointedly moves from scene to scene with Imagist rapidity. Reading contemporary narrative poems, one often feels an enervating awkwardness and verbosity of their exposition; *The Diviners*, however, unfolds with narrative speed and assurance. This is the way, one instinctively feels, that a long narrative poem should move after a century of both movies and Modernism.

McDowell has handled another aspect of the long poem differently from most modern American writers. He lets his plot stretch across time. The Twentieth-century narrative poem has generally built its plot around either a single lyric moment or a closely related group of lyric moments. Such narrative poems might be described as *vertical*—the weight of the story rests on a focused temporal point. The plot of Jeffers's "Roan Stallion," for instance, focuses mostly on the violent events of a single night. Most of Frost's mid-length narratives unfold in a single episode even if they frequently allude to earlier events. *The Diviners* works in a radically different way. Its narrative design is *horizontal*; the plot spans five decades and encompasses two generations. The narrative material is not fussy, refined, or conventionally poetic; rather it is sprawling, ambitious, and unembarrassed by the often vulgar concerns of its characters. How refreshing it is to read a narrative poem that doesn't apologize for telling a story but trusts its own substance to command our attention. The sheer momentum of the story carries readers over rough spots that might upset a less dynamic narrative. *The Diviners* operates in a genre that today one associates almost entirely with prose or film—the family saga. It resembles works like *The Wapshot Chronicle*, *The Custom of the Country*, *The Magnificent Ambersons*, or *Padre Padrone* more closely than culture epics like *A*, *Gunslinger*, *Paterson* or *The Cantos*. In this way McDowell unabashedly reappropriates the basic privilege of the novelist—to tell the human stories of his time and place. Yet for all its narrative thrust, *The Diviners* remains palpably poetic, even if its lyric turns as often come in the evocative juxtapositions between scenes as in the scenes themselves.

McDowell has a sure sense of setting up a scene or character with a few quick strokes. Once you have read the opening section, reread the first page, which successfully introduces four characters in a little over thirty lines. McDowell has mastered Hemingway's trick of providing no more than the few details necessary to evoke a character. The son, for example, is described initially only in a handful of scattered comments by his mother. Her remarks—half worries, half complaints— tell us both about his brainy isolation and her disregard for his peculiar gifts. McDowell's descriptions often cut both ways—skewering two characters at once. His technique is noticeably cinematic, but it compresses action more radically than a film would. I have never seen a narrative poem move the way *The Diviners* does; it is quick, assured, and effective. Reinventing the rules of the form, McDowell has found an arresting and innovative way to sustain a book-length poem. As a poet, I could not resist making careful notes on McDowell's narrative technique, and I suspect *The Diviners* will prove influential among young writers for its surprising solutions to the problems of the long poem.

A certain type of literary reader may criticize *The Diviners* because it matter-of-factly presents middle class characters caught in the crises of domestic existence. What could be more unredeemably mundane than "Boss," the father, who is so lost in his own career that he can only offer his family money in place of love and attention? What setting could be less overtly evocative than a nameless white-collar suburb of Los Angeles in the calm 1950s? McDowell willfully ignores the genteel conventions of contemporary long poems not only by exploring the lives of quotidian individuals but also by discovering genuine passion and pathos in their lives. The cast of *The Diviners* are not characters one meets in a poem by James Merrill or Richard Howard, but they are people one encounters every day in jobs, schools, and neighborhoods. Their lives represent an unexplored region of contemporary poetry, and it is fascinating to see what McDowell makes of them. He is both compassionate and merciless. He takes his characters seriously enough to explore their troubled lives without reaching for easy resolutions. He bears the uncomfortable knowledge that most unhappiness and failure cannot be corrected—an uneasy insight that is an anathema to our sentimental, upbeat age. He understands the contradictory impulses at the center of the human heart. Most important, he never condescends to his characters, even those he dislikes. He has developed the novelist's skill of portraying characters sympathetically without forgiving them their trespasses. Ambitious, unconventional, and intentionally disquieting, *The Diviners* is one of the most absorbing and original long poems of recent years.

For the idols have spoken vanity, and the diviners
have seen a lie, and have told false dreams.

Zecharia 10:2

Sometimes I wonder if this be the world
We live in, or the world that lives in us.

E. A. Robinson

CHAPTER ONE

They waded in . . .

THE FIFTIES

When Al and his career were very young,
Before the nickname, Boss, was pinned on him,
He had to spend most weekdays far from home.
From Chicago or New York he'd call the house
To say goodnight and talk with his only son,
Who hated phones, the voices trapped in them.
The distance from his homelife gnawed at Al,
Whose own dad had forsaken family.
He thought of this as Eleanor, his wife,
Discussed the day's events and hung up lonely.
Dissatisfied, she spent long nervous nights
Until the Open House in '58.
Her son, who was eight, had begged her to attend.
"Why not?" she said.
                              She parked in the visitor's lot
And stepped out of her Edsel like a queen,
Or so it seemed to her son who was watching her
From a window in his homeroom science class.
Her ankle bracelet sparkled in black-top heat;
Her red hair caught the sun and softened it.
The teacher felt soft, too, when she strolled in.

"I couldn't miss our little Einsteins' Day,"
She said. "You must be Mr. ..."
                              "Just call me Bill."
The teacher led her up the nearest aisle
So he could show the tar pits diorama
And brag about her son's accomplishment.

"Your Tom," he said, "was in charge of animals.
They're realistic—scary—don't you think?"

"He reads a lot," she said. The boy, embarrassed,
Fell back to watch a girl with scalpel in hand
About to probe and slice a cow's brown eye,
While at the tar pits Eleanor rubbed the fang
Of a sabertooth depicted going down.

"They thought the stuff was water, right?" she said.
Bill nodded.
                    "It looked inviting. They waded in—"

"And got sucked down." She finished his sentence for him.
The way she said it, especially that word,
Made Bill's knees buckle. He leaned on the table for balance
And silently cursed himself. Hair flat with sweat,
His face was red from holding in his gut.
He felt inadequate, desire's fool.
He wondered what to say to keep her there.
He took a chance.
                    "May I call you Eleanor?
It's funny but I feel we've met before."

She caught the hint and laughed.
                    "We're meeting now."
Bill thought of undoing the zipper of her dress
As he steered her up and down the classroom rows.
She liked his graying temples and blue eyes,
The perspiration veil above his lip;
She hesitated as they reached the door.
"I'm free for dinner later, if you'd like."
The look between them settled any doubts.

4

From then on Tom spent many TV nights
With sitters while his mother stayed out late.
In haste she'd pat his hair, explain the meeting
She couldn't miss that night, then close her door
To begin the hour of bathing and getting dressed.
But Tom could press his ear against the wall,
And later even lie down on her bed
And imagine mother singing just for him.

TOM:

The first thing I remember: my dad is gone.
Not permanent, but enough to rattle me.
My mother works all day, then rushes home
To change and go. The sitters are mostly ok,
But I prefer my room with lots of books.
Mom gets home late. Some mornings when it's dark
I sneak into her bed. I touch her face.
I get this feeling. I touch her and I hurt.

ELEANOR:

My boy hides in his room, says he's preparing.
He locks the door and I must shake the knob
And yell Go Out and Play! I get all weepy,
Never what I want. A horn sounds off
Outside on the gravel drive. I stare at the mirror.
My make-up could be better. I poke my hair
And stand, then pull my sweater down and go,
Imagining Bill's hands exploring there.
Then Tom unlocks his door and watches me.
I peck him on the forehead, hurry past;
I'm thinking Damn Him, meaning everyone.

TOM:

The screen door slams. I lock my door again.
I study notes and pull out all my books
On polar exploration; I memorize
The characters, events, all dates and charts.
I prepare for when I'm older, more important,
Maybe President. Or I may leave.
It must be cold outside the galaxy,
But knowing about Admiral Scott will help.

Al slams his office door. He works the phone,
And says hello as he loosens the knot of his tie.

"I got your name and number from a pal
Who says you used to be a cop in Frisco.
He says you're good at finding what gets lost.
I'm on the road a lot, and so's my wife.
You follow me? That's right. I want to know.
I'll come by after lunch if that's ok."

At 1:00 a cab drops Al at Mission and Fourth.
He pauses, pulls a matchbook from his vest,
And double-checks the address, then lets it drop
Beside a leaflet hawking Stevenson,
He crosses traffic, making drivers stop,
Then bulls up varnished stairs and raps his fist
On frosted glass. He peppers the door again.
A voice inside shouts
                          "Open! Come on in!"
Inside a woman looks up from her desk
And says "Sit down." Al wrinkles in a chair.
O'Hara, who was writing, drops her pen.

"Ok," she says, "suppose you fill me in."

Al fidgets with his hands and rambles on
About his company, his working wife,
His quiet son who won't get close enough,
The deadening weeks of travel coast to coast,
Temptations he's turned down at swank hotels.
O'Hara lets him talk. She studies him,
And now and then makes notes on a pocket pad:

> Al's wife—Eleanor—30. Clothes designer/58 Pacific
> Ave. One kid—Tom—8. Guy on road/gal on town.
> Out when he calls/nervous when questioned/moody/
>   headaches
> every night. Description: 5'8"/125/red hair (long)/
> green eyes/snappy dresser (naturally). Photo in hand.
> Tail and shoot.

As Al winds down he wheezes like a patient.
"Are you a drinking man?" O'Hara asks,
And pulls a fifth of bourbon from a drawer.
Red splotches form a pattern on Al's face
And down the sides of his neck. He rubs his eyes,
And in the voice of a little boy says
                                    "Please."

        "Let's eat up in the hills tonight," Bill says.
"You know. That spot my mother liked so much.
Romantic. We'll be inspired by the view."
Inspired is what he needs, for he was up late
Last night, hungering for sympathy.
He wants to put an end to it, his feeling
That every room intends to spit him out.
But she has troubles, too, and wants to talk.

"At work two models got the clap and quit.
The customs agents seized our Paris furs.
We'll lose their eastern buyers...while I gain weight."
Disgusted, Eleanor scoots her salad plate
Beyond the range of her fork. "And then there's home.
If Tom knew how we meet he'd disappear,
And Al—" she laughs—"If Al found out he'd kill us."

Bill reaches for her hand, but she withdraws it.
He lowers his voice, measuring what he says—
The seductive voice he's learned from teaching books.
"Why don't you leave? You could move in with me."

She nods and smiles, then puts it simply enough:
"Move in. With Tom, I suppose? And on your salary?
And Al—you think he'd go along with that?
Just sit by, pay the movers and wish us well?"

"I guess you think he'd throw us down the stairs."

"Not just," she says. "He'd want to hurt us first."
Then neither speaks, but both are thinking

Why?

Why am I here? This situation's wrong;
It's dangerous but fun, and I can't stop it.

O'Hara signals the waiter and pays up fast.
She waves the change away. "It's yours," she says,
And hustles through the piano bar for the door.
Outside she aims her camera and shoots.
The couple in focus kiss beside a car,
A tender shot, then climb inside and go.

O'Hara starts her car and follows them
As they head east into the purple hills.
The moon is full tonight, and O'Hara works
At shooting rolls and rolls of evidence.
At last the rocking car she targets slows
And calms itself. The lovers' hands appear.
The woman in the lens sits up, adjusts
The rearview mirror and works her lipstick hand.

At work the following day a card arrives
For Eleanor.
                    "Let's talk," O'Hara says,
And flashes the photographs. "You know what's here."
The only sound that Eleanor can make
Is *why*? "Your husband paid," O'Hara says.
"I've got to report, but I'll say the film's no good.
The man's ambitious. I'll give him points for that,
But he's going nowhere I would want to be."

        One night Bill zones out, staring past his knees
On which he balances his students' themes.
The grading and writing of remarks is long
On a Sunday night. His penny loafers are scuffed,
Symbolic of the way he feels each day
Before ill-mannered classes. His former wife
Once said he'd never leave his science room.
For years he thought she'd diagnosed him well,
Then Eleanor appeared to prove her wrong.
He'd violated the Scientist's Code that day,
Disturbing substances he couldn't grasp.
He knew it, too, but turned away from years
Of operating as he'd learned to do.

Bill comes back to the present, rubs his face,
And enters blue TV across the room.
The sound is off, allowing him to read
Or think as he pleases.
                          "Touch the phone," he says,
And he does so thinking of Eleanor, of meals
Together, then parking and rocking in the hills.

A gangster movie opens on the screen
And Bill forgets the phone. The papers slip
And spread out on the carpet stained with use.
He only faintly hears the car outside,
The gravel crunched by tires. Still concentrating
On the screen, he glances quickly through the curtains.
Reluctantly he moves out of TV.
Two Hammer Men in suits approach the house,
Resembling men he's watching in the film.
He shakes his head, attempting to sever the link
Between the TV drama and his life,
But the men outside are pounding on his door.

So open it, he thinks, *and take what comes.*

He does. The visitors are on him fast,
Abusing him, efficient mute machines.
Bill sees his class, his distant, former wife,
A peeled cow's eye dissected on a table.
When they break his legs he hears his one loud cry
Despite the rag he gags on. Then Eleanor,
The gently rocking car, insistent, yes,
Their lives constricted, then colliding, numb.

Tom tries to hear his father through the wall,
That voice a storm of random, painful words.
How long? and *Why?* the building thunder asks.
The world, his mother, doesn't answer back.
Just sing! her son commands, to make it right!
But nothing comes of it. Alone, afraid,
Tom sings off key a favorite lullabye.
The morning light is gray, the room is cold,
The thunder builds across the desolate hall.
At last Tom hears his mother's voice on fire;
The thunder crashes, footsteps rattle the hall,
A door creaks on its hinges, then slams shut.

Some awful moments pass, then father comes,
His sweaty face so pitiful and cruel
Tom wants to kiss and slap it all at once.
Instead he cries and leans into a hug.

"Where's Mom," he says into his father's shirt.
Al says,
                "Forget about your school today.
Come out with me. Let's talk. At the kitchen table
Al caps the sugar bowl and wrestles with grief
He thinks his son could never understand.

"Where's Mom?" Tom says again. He's calmer now,
But only outwardly. Al studies him.

"Your mother's ill," he says. "She's gone away."

"How long?" Tom asks.
                            "Until she's right again.
A couple of days, a week. It won't be long."

"I want to go with her," Tom says. Al acts
As if he doesn't hear, but shakes his head
Like some slow, final pendulum. Tom cries.

"There, there," Al says. "I've got good news for you.
You know the school I went to as a boy?
You transfer there tomorrow. Happy now?"

Tom blubbers, wiping his sleeve across his nose
And says, "But I don't have a uniform."

"I'll pick it up today. A blazer and slacks.
You'll look just like I do each day at work."

So Eleanor departs the galaxy,
Or so Tom thinks as he keeps time in his room
And writes long notes from books on Admiral Scott.
He wonders if she'll starve, be forced to kill
A dog and eat it raw. He wants to grow
Be shrewd and fast, outrun his loneliness
And bring his mother home. The North is far.

But Eleanor drives southeast, somewhere, follows
The two-lane desert road through small motels.
Her room seems always smaller than a car,
But first things first. She lights a cigarette,
Then sits down on the bed to count her money.
The counting is not long, she notices,
Which means some grunt work sooner than she'd like.
She misses Tom and wonders about Bill—
Their luck had turned on them, that's why she ran.

It's what she tells herself as she unpacks.
She hesitates, then reaches for the phone.
Al says hello. He listens. He hangs up.
Eleanor cries, decides to take a shower,
Then grab some sleep with a nudge from seconal.

For half-a-year the pattern repeats itself
As Eleanor crisscrosses the bleak Southwest.
One month she deals blackjack in Las Vegas,
Or pushes drinks in Bisbee, types in Austin.
In Santa Fe she's fired for drinking too much.
Her money thin, her prospects all played out,
She calls again and says she's coming home.
Al hears the liquor in her voice and smiles,
And tells her not so fast.
                              "I filed last month,"
He says to no immediate reply.
"I asked for custody, but I'll drop it all
If you agree to fix yourself and stay."

Exhausted, bitter, Eleanor agrees.

        In treatment, she has very far to go.
Submitting to hypnosis, Eleanor
Relives the early years of life with Al:

        I sipped my coffee in the breakfast room
        And stared at the wild roses winding high
        Above the house, tangled in a tree.
        Al said (so eager to please me, so intense),
        "For you I'll cut them down. Just say the word."

I'd hear his scissors working nervously,
Their sound like his voice talking to itself
About a secret past. He scared me then,
His pent up, innocent arrogance and fear.
So I withdrew while he began to travel.
I see now he retreated, too, but to work.
Except for Tom, we made a botch of it.

The session ends and she retreats into sleep.
The next day, sitting listless in the sun,
She manages to write some lines to Tom:

Sometimes I wake up laughing I am so happy.
Sometimes I feel the sun. Then I am humble,
A little sad. And I am with you, Love.

CHAPTER TWO

A storm of learning . . .

THE SIXTIES

"Just tell me what to say in my report,"
Says Tom. Al swirls the coffee in his Answer Cup
And tables his spoon.
                    "Ok," he says, "what class?"

"It's history again," Tom sighs. "I'm stumped."

He feels most like a grain of cereal.
"I hate the subject," says the shrinking boy
As Eleanor walks in with a photo album.

"What subject do you hate?" she wants to know,
Then focuses on glossy 8 x 10s.
Al rubs his jaw and asks,
                    "What period?"

"The Forties. Shoulder pads," says Eleanor.

"You mean," Al says, "those styles that hide the fact
A woman's got no build beneath the tent."

"The concept works for fat men, too," she says,
A bit too cheerily. Al rubs his gut.

"I'm helping Tom," he says. "Don't bother us."

"I thought you asked about my show," she says.
Corrected, she looks down and does not speak
As Tom feels dark.
                    "It's open," he replies,
And Al, as if conducting an interview,
Proceeds to tell his son what he must do.

"Then write about the after-baby boom,"
He says, "when mothers spent more energy
Making careers instead of families."
As Al breathes in, a laugh escapes his wife,
One clear sharp cackle rising from her book.

"Was that the latest speech at Rotary?"
She asks. The lines cut deeper in their faces
As Al gives her a look that says *Don't Push*.
Tom speaks up fast to sidetrack them.
                              "But where am I?"

Recovered, Al says "We're talking your own time.
You're old enough to read the papers, boy.
Get started now. The out-of-luck are growing.
The money-makers muscle up. That's me,
You know, and some day you'll be joining me.
Just study business, Tom, and get the degree.
There's other things, of course—the way you dress,
The car you drive. Make sure you pay as you go,
And when you marry, get the family,
Then settle down in a one-color neighborhood."
Al stands and tosses coffee down his throat.
"They call me Boss at work. You earn that name.
Well, getting old just means you own more things.
It's time to go."
                    Tom silently agrees.

At recess, Tom drops out of the kickball game
And drifts unobserved behind a bungalow.
The Brothers' lessons trumpet in his head,
A storm of learning shut out with a deck
Of his father's cards he shuffles over and over.
They make a sound like someone's dying breath;
It comforts Tom, and when his mind is blank
He stills the deck and turns cards one by one.
He's half-way through the suits before the King
of Diamonds freezes in his trembling hand.
He tilts that monetary face against
The flat, disabling sun and wills the card
To erupt in fire, but no divine help comes.
So Tom takes out his matches, tilts the card,
And leans its hardened edge against the flame.
Just as the king's face curls and vanishes,
A Brother's shadow drops, screens out the sun.

Tom's next tough hours are spent on a rickety stool
In front of the class. The girls, especially,
Make google eyes at him. They hope he'll blush,
But Tom sits straitbacked, gazing at the sun.
If he could wish his parents gone he might;
Instead they meet for lunch not far away.

"The quiche is soggy," Eleanor complains,
And jabs a fleck of spinach 'round her plate.

"You ought to try red meat," her husband says,
Attacking an oozing slab of porterhouse.
She manages a smile and says aloud,

"You're certainly enjoying every bite."

Al thinks the brittle brightness in her eyes
Encouragement enough (or all he'll get);
An ice bucket appears, and dry champagne.
Al answers Eleanor's uncertain look.

"It's April first, our anniversary."

The blooming seed of panic in her gut
Prompts Eleanor to rise, excusing herself.
When she returns, composed, her hand remains
As Al's own covers it.

                    "I've loved you, Hon."
The tears in his eyes won't fall, she notices.
Oh, that's too bad, she thinks, then *that's pathetic*,
Then her own sadness surfaces and spreads,
A stain that even Al might one day see.
She wonders how the mark has touched their son,
Then shakes the thought, unable to cope with it.
With too much haste they drain the champagne dry,
Reach back through talk to less encumbered days
And even feel affection stir once more,
Beginners with all of time ahead of them.
Out in the car they kiss like newlyweds.
Excited, Al proposes a Bridal Suite
And Eleanor is willing, naming the Biltmore.
She scoots across the seat to lean on him
But feels the barrier rise up again,
Not knowing that the name of the hotel
Has panicked Al, who fumbles for his keys
And glances at his watch.

                    "Oh, damn!" he says.
"Forgive me. There's a meeting I forgot.
I have to go."

              "What else is new?" she says,

And moves back to her own side of the car,
A place where she can tune out, watching signs.
Al prays she doesn't question his change of heart.
He knows he's missed an opportunity
For tenderness that might dissolve their grudge.
Fat chance, he tells himself, and feels relieved
That he's dodged the hotel staff addressing him
By name in front of Eleanor. *I've quit,*
He tells himself, but that's not good enough.
If Eleanor knew he'd been with other women
She'd run him through the courts. She'd make him pay.
Or so he tells himself. What could be worse?

       After school Tom says "Let's miss the bus"
To a pudgy twelve-year-old from Baldwin Park.

"For what?" the dim one asks.
                        "For another life."
Tom's friend begins to sweat but lets himself
Be led down many blocks to a dead-end street,
To a creaking gate that opens toward the door
Of Mrs. Junius Hope's abandoned house.

"Not here!" Tom's heavy partner whines and squirms.
"The place is haunted. That's why it's boarded up.
They say she was a witch, that she killed her husband."

"Our parents say those things to keep us out,"
Tom says. "I want to find out what they know,
And so do you."
                Obedient, his friend
Climbs up and wrestles through an open window.
Inside he rubs his knees and fights the darkness
For a glimpse of Tom. The rotting parlor stinks,

And he considers scrambling back outside,
But as he turns Tom holds him by the collar.

"In here," Tom whispers, "see what I just found!"
In a dark back room Tom brings from the closet shelf
A stack of stained and dusty photographs.
Tom smiles as he picks through them, choosing one
To show his friend. The other boy looks down
And blushes. His eyes get big. He laughs like a horse.

"Let's see some more!" he says and grabs the rest.
Forgetting where he is, forgetting the hour,
The timid boy gets lost in Mrs. Hope.
"I heard my mother say she slept with the mayor.
I heard that's why she left. He paid her off
Because she said she'd tell all on TV."

"I heard she was selling drugs to high school kids,"
Tom says. His friend says

                    "Maybe she did both.
These pictures are amazing! Look at this!"

But Tom looks past his friend's excited hand
As if he heard his name from far away.
He leans out of the room, into the hall,
While his friend continues studying each shot
And groaning softly, shaking in his knees.
When Tom steps back to grab his friend's damp arm
The nervous boy is startled, dropping the photos—
Tom pulls him to the landing, points downstairs.

Below, a figure in a dull green coat
Moves quickly from a cloakroom near the door.
The figure mutters to itself and stops

Before a grimy mirror. Sobbing once
It whirls and catches both boys cowering;
They want to run but want much more to see.
The boys retreat inside the snapshot room,
The figure coming two steps at a time.
It blocks the door, its breathing quick and hard.
A heavy scarf is quickly pulled away
And there before them, looking beautiful,
The subject of the photos comes to life.
Tom looks at the floor. He shuffles nervously
And paws a lick of hair down on his head;
She tongues the palm of her hand and touches him there.
Tom's friend forgets to breathe and turns bright red.

"Relax," she tells him with a wicked smile,
"You see I'm not a ghost. It's hot in here
But the window's stuck." She steps out of her coat
And turning drops it on the bannister.
Returning to the room she sees the pictures
All jumbled at the feet of the heavy boy.
She stoops to pack them in a pile and sorts
Them as she rises. Her eyes are moons on fire,
Her laugh is like a bell. She stares at herself,
Then looking up she nails the gawking boys.
"You think they're dirty? Think I look ok?
Come show me all the shots you like the most."
The boys move back, but only by a step.

"He found them!" the big boy blusters. "He made me come!"

The woman looks amused.
                              "He made you what?
I think you two should come downstairs with me.
It's cooler there. The three of us can talk.

I'll tell you why I closed my house up tight;
You'll tell me all the dirty things you've heard,
And what you hoped to find." She notices
How both boys stare at the tightness of her jeans.
She pulls her tank-top out and airs herself.
They sweat, they ache, they follow her downstairs.

        While Tom discovers Hope in a gloomy house,
The afternoon drags on for Eleanor.
A meeting with her business partner breaks
And she is out the door, ignoring calls
From buyers in the east who don't approve
The new designs she spent last season on.
An unlucky year so far—the Saks account,
The Magnin people, too, have all been lost.
Her partner whines about his mortgages,
His alimony, his kids who hate his guts,
Her absurd designs, his life in jeopardy,
And all of it her fault. He wants her gone.

If only it were easy, she tells herself.
If only I could wish myself away
And wake up rested in another life.
Come on. You tried that once.
                                        She makes herself
Recall her aimless trek from town to town
As summer and her prospects all dried up.
Then home to Tom, to try again with Al,
To divert the randomness of surging time
To one coherent pattern she might trust.
Now years from that resolve, at Miramar

She claims a booth-for-one behind the bar.
She checks her watch, she wipes her mouth and drinks,
Her face a blank that clouds with interference.
Through many drinks she studies her designs
That let her down, then calmly rips them up.
The bartender notes the familiar, listless way
That Eleanor nods her head. He keeps his distance;
He waters down her refills, and when she goes
He shrugs and sighs while pocketing his tip.
It's adequate. He drops her from his mind.

Behind the wheel she has more time to kill
And turns the radio on for company.
A momentary keening, intimate,
Gives way to voices pitching clothes and cars,
Hawaiian and Las Vegas trips for two,
The specials of some local dinner joints.
The voices' unobstructed eagerness
Remind her most of Al, the way he talks
And bullies through the day, compressing hours
As he might mash an orange between his hands.
The maddening advertising impulse crests,
Abruptly crashes into song and dies.
She rubs the dial to off and concentrates,
With little luck, on emptying her mind.
On a residential El Sereno street
She parks in the shade, observing their first house,
Where Tom was born. The place looks smaller now;
The exterior needs paint, the lawn is shabby,
But the gravel drive and railroad tracks remain.
She sits there crying as the sun goes down.

* * *

The decade drowns in violence and blood,
Conspiracies and unacknowledged coups.
The nation seems to lie down willingly
As Tom gets older, filling up with grief.
The faces and the land ahead look bleak,
And he begins to hear about the war.
Desolated, angrier each day,
He'd like to kill. A war is one good way.

But some nights when he's quiet in his room
Tom eases up, a silent, grief-grown boy,
An inarticulate and bitter boy.
If his dad could only talk it out with him—
But he is like the Main Street Cinema
Since 1965—always dark.
Tom's sense of loss and pain won't dissipate
As he focuses more and more on TV death,
So easy to watch bland heroes sprawled in blood.

One night a puzzling feeling moves in him;
The hero-grief he feels is not unlike
The nervous ecstasy of Mrs. Hope.
By saying this out loud he feels relieved,
Though why he does he can't begin to grasp.
Perspiring, grateful for Mrs. Hope, he sleeps
And dreams of that day's battering at school.

To live is easy, the way the Brothers tell it,
But home again, far from the Word of Life,
Tom hates his bit part in the life itself.
At meals he sees his father wolf down food
Then lumber to the den, to stacked reports
He'll rule the boardroom with. The evening goes
While Tom turns on TV and enters news,

Observing prime-time streets not far away
Where men and women hunker down in boxes,
The thinnest veils against a winter blow.
Some ice up in their rags, turning blue
Like painted porcelain; some light up trash
While others dog the steps of laundered suits,
Requesting one small slice of their good luck.
The losers lick their chops, dreaming of meat.

Then all turn up together in a TV church.
A waxy, pompous man with lacquered hair
Patrols their hearts with microphone in hand,
His wholesome choir waiting in the wings.
The hymns are beautiful, the speaker weeps,
And money fills convenient silver bowls.
Tom rises, trying to shout the speaker down,
Then squirms awake. The anthem on TV
Becomes a field of brain-dead static gray.
He mutes the sound, and these lines come to him:

> *If you're walking on the west side of this town*
> *At 4:00 A.M., remember that the streets*
> *Belong to the cops, the garbage men, and me.*

CHAPTER THREE

*A fear so sweet and
thorough . . .*

THE SEVENTIES

The lottery, with Vietnam the prize,
Takes place for Tom in 1971.
In the college cafeteria he squirms
Beside the others sweating out the draw.
If they could gaze into the months ahead
They'd see their roster cut, some figures fading. . .

Like the kid from Little Rock who'll fall on his cot,
Then drop from earth when a shell explodes his hut;
Like Clem, the unofficial pharmacist,
Who in a fire fight will take three rounds
But stay alive enough to crawl a mile
Through bamboo as thick as cotton in a bottle;
Like Frank who read and wrote his own escape
Out of the barrio of East L.A.,
Who will never see the tunnel open up
Behind him on patrol, the boy lean out
And squeeze the trigger of his captured rifle;
Like Ernie, left wing photojournalist
And active campus speaker against the war—
He'll sacrifice this life for Canada—
A wasted missing number like the rest.

Of course, the boys can't know the roles they'll act
As Tom turns up the TV sound in time
To hear his number—fifty—called out twice.
The look on Ernie's face makes Tom afraid,
A fear so sweet and thorough he feels sick.

"That's rotten," Jerry says, whose own high number
Had been announced before. "I'd trade with you."

"Like hell," Tom says. "You care but you're not stupid."

"You sorry shit," Clem says, "take two of these.
Oh, hell, take four. What difference does it make."

Tom cups his hands for pills and pops the bunch
And chases them with water. The TV screen
Becomes a face he'd like to bayonet.
He wonders why. Why is this happening?
He shakes his head and says "I just won't go."

"You got it," Ernie says. "Let's hitch up north.
I know where we can get some new ID."

"I'm staying here," Tom says. "I'll go C.O."

"Good luck," Clem laughs. "You know how tough that is?
You've got to be a saint or priest to get it."

But Tom is plotting, listing in his mind
The names of people he'll ask letters of:
His childhood priest, his high school principal,
The women on his street whose lawns he mowed.

Three months go by, he passes his physical,

And then the draft board hearing date arrives.
Five fleshy gray men look up from their files
As Tom comes in prepared for questions like

What happens when a tank attacks your mother?
What happens when the enemy prevails?

Since anything he'd say would be a lie,
Tom figures that telling any lie will do.
Instead, he's told they've granted his appeal.
The letters, ten of them, have made a case
That no one on the Board cares to dispute.

Tom wanders from the building like a patient,
And in the park, alone, he burns the day.

     Al shuts his study door. He sits up late
With scotch and smoke and wonders what went wrong.
His boy, up north somewhere, is picketing
Against the draft. Where does the kid get off?
Himself a veteran of World War II,
He thinks of duty, pride, then flares with shame.
"If your country calls, then you just have to go,"
Al says to no one in the thickening room.
The drink unlocks a barred door in his head
And Al is uniformed and young again,
About to splash ashore in France and kill
For the first time. He flattens on the sand,
Takes aim and squeezes off some nervous shots;
A boy beside him drops, and when he can
Al rolls the victim over on his side
To see a face much younger than his own.
The body seems to sink into the sand,
The helium of spirit escaping it.
Al thinks of his own dying as a secret
That some blonde soldier is about to tell;
He cannot shake the cold that enters him.

It's after three when Eleanor comes down
To cap the bottle, rinse the ashtray out
And shake Al from the beach back to his life.
He fancies that he hears his name somewhere;
His wife sneaks into shadows he can't clear
As snipers open up on every side. . .
The nightmare's membrane separates and spreads,
Releasing him. Al looks at Eleanor
And slowly rubs the age back in his face.
His troubles are too great to solve tonight.
Obedient, he follows her up to bed.

    While father snores and thrashes against the night,
While mother lights a candle, thinking of Tom,
And keeps watch to make sure the wick is trimmed,
In fog in Oakland Tom waits for a bus,
Which rolls into the depot after dawn.
Three soldiers muscle duffel bags down steps,
Their faces glazed, then animate with joy
As open arms and weeping cover them.
For one stone instant, Tom sees in their faces
The torment of this birth, the bus as war's womb,
And down its steps the world.
                              Duane appears.
He hesitates, as if he needs more time
To realign his heart and head with peace,
Then spots his college buddy in the crowd,
Descends and hugs Tom hard enough to wind him.
Duane steps back and flicks at Tom's long hair.

"That's sweet," he says. "Won any contests yet?"

"Well look at you! With a decoration, too!"

Tom snaps at the purple heart above the breast,
Then shoulders the duffel bag. They cross the bridge
To normalcy, a drinker's drunk in North Beach.
Through many rounds they toast departed friends.
Duane takes all the time he needs to tell
About his work, his time in hospital,
The fear that he had lost his only face,
The priest who sat down, nodding mechanically,
His body like the ticking of a clock,
His promise that Duane was going home.

All night they wander, losing big at cards
And in and out of twenty-minute rooms;
At one Duane unclasps his purple heart
And pins it on a dress, a souvenir.
At dawn they stare at Alcatraz from the wharf.
Tom thinks of what a castle it would make,
How his dad would be the perfect lord of it.

> *...It's a battered old suitcase*
> *to a hotel someplace,*
> *and a wound that will never heal...*

A year goes by, and from many miles away
A song Tom favors purls in his mother's sleep.
In bed she lets her mind work as it will,
Imagines crew-cut Tom, a boy of eight
Beside her make-up mirror as she becomes
A lipstick girl for dinner in the hills.
She knows he's worried, wishing she would stay,
So Eleanor begins to sing for him
Through the backward-looking surface of the mirror:

> *Waltzing Matilda, waltzing Matilda*
> *you'll go a-waltzing Matilda with me. . .*

The boy calms down, watching, listening,
A rapture that will last until she goes.

Al tosses under the sheet and breaks the spell,
And Eleanor moves out from bed to chair
To look at what the years have made of her,
Discovering in the mirror their signature.

"You've done it to yourself," she says aloud.
"The business won your heart, and gladly ate it.
Not that you would have saved some part for Al
If you had known, but Tom deserved your love.
You didn't give enough."
                              The glassed-in suspect
Is nervous as accuser and accused
Lay out make-up, their hands in unison.
Mechanically, to each side of their face,
They apply a little brush and reappear.

Much later when the brash alarm goes off,
Al grabs his robe and stumbles down the hall.
From side to side he bumps against the walls,
Then finds his wife and coffee on the porch.
His eyes are eggs with tracer-lines of blood.

"We need to bring Tom home," says Eleanor.

"I know," says Al before he gives it thought,
And as he does he also means *what for?*
The blood backs up, begins to color him.
"What's that you're reading? What happened to your face?"
As Eleanor looks up with heavy eyes,
Al feels he's on the run inside himself.

"I'm reading Tom's old letters."

"He wrote damn few,"
Says Al.

"He wrote enough," says Eleanor.
"You never took the time to read them close
Because you couldn't see your life in his."

"That isn't fair," Al says.

"Perhaps it's not.
I've done my share of looking elsewhere, too.
But if we ask, he'll come back home to us."

Al does not speak. He thinks *and then what happens?*
But Eleanor has entered the letters again.
Al grouses in the shower, thinking of Tom
And Eleanor's new face. He snaps the soap.

Tom lies back on his bed, a prisoner
Of the ceiling flocked to look like cottage cheese.
No light is on and fog dilutes the sun.
The rapping on the door, the smokey voice,
Occur just as he has imagined them—
The summons to a dismal obligation.

"What is it now?" he asks without delight.

"Come out here, Son, and talk to me," Al says.

Tom steps out in the hall and follows him
As if condemned, the victim of a tunnel.
Al waves Tom to a kitchen chair.

He waits.

"You know, you've been back home for several weeks,
And don't you think it's time you got to work?"

"I have," Tom says. "I monitor the war."

Al leans back in his chair. He rolls his eyes,
Then tilting forward shakes his moneyed head.
"I don't want that to sidetrack us again,"
He says. "You've got some personal beliefs,
But there's the real world, too. You follow me?"
Tom thinks of how their roads have just converged.

"I bet you have a plan," he says. "Let's hear it."

"You may feel as if you've come home from a war,
But I found out that war was in work, too.
Don't buy the bull that says you ought to work
At what you love." Tom caps the sugar bowl
As Al goes on. "I want you to work for me."

"I thought I might go back for my degree."

"Forget that schoolroom junk. You're past it now.
The fabric market's booming. I need you there."

Tom lightly pricks the table with a knife.
You've got to make a move, he tells himself
And wonders how his marching brought him here.

"No warehouse work," Tom says, "and what's my pay?"

"I'm thinking ten to start. That good enough?"

"You'd better up it five, include a car,

And four weeks off with pay."
                                    Al rubs the wrinkles
On his forehead. He agrees, he circles Tom
And claps him on the shoulder, saying Son
And feeling in that instant as if God
Himself were leaning down to slap his back.
"And one thing more. You'll give me an advance.
I need a place that's bigger than that room."

"You might look into something close to home—
To satisfy your mother. Think it over."

Tom does but in the end decides on distance,
Occasions with long silences between.
The weekdays pass, Tom learns his father's trade
And steadily moves up to keep accounts.
His boy inside the company frees Al,
Who has more time for the lodge and rounds of golf
While after work Tom breathes the Westwood air
Out on his narrow deck. He drinks alone
And works the books until they come out right,
And paces sums and drinks with cigarettes,
And keeps time by the ashtrays filling up.
But tonight, stubbing out a Camel Light,
He rubs his chest and sighs for company.
The Bar Night calls. He grabs his coat and goes.

The wind lies down in Santa Monica,
But not the restless, hungry for a fix
Of some exotic, rough experience.

Tom walks the esplanade from drink to drink,
But nothing startles like the black girl's face
Above Kahlúa in a corner booth.
Despite himself he does a doubletake;
He drops his smokes, then asks if he can sit,
And after introductions questions her.

Elaine has spent years working for the poor,
Attempting to bring back the neighborhood
That died before her parents settled there.
Delighted, talking till two, they close the club
And make a date for dinner the following night.
Back home Tom thinks of phoning Eleanor.
He smiles. It's late. Besides, what would he say?
He goes to bed and dreams of Africa,
The shameful war, his work, the girl he wants.

When time allows they meet for drinks or dinner
Or walks along the beach when the weather's warm,
Until they finally arrive at Tom's
To lie down with each other near a fire,
Pressing into each other before some word
Intrudes to block and keep them separate.
They know the counter-arguments; they choose,
Rejecting sins that sew one generation
To the next.
                "We'll both climb out of that," she says.

"Just kiss me till I quit the company,"
Tom says, "then walk out in the day with me."
She covers up his mouth to soothe his nerves,
Then says
                "We'll try to live as long as we can,
Then die with as little pain as possible."

"That's possible," Tom says, yet wonders how.

Tom rises early, rehearsing what he'll say
To his bleak associates, their pasty faces
Shining in their polished gold tie bars.
His father's face, his boss, reflects back, too,
And that is the glare that makes him look away.
Tom thinks of other names for lies: long bows
And gally floppers, windies, whoppers. He curses,
Imagining that the boys he'll soon address
Might snap with jealousy. He sees how they
Might truss his hands and feet with electric cord;
He imagines the gag of someone's handkerchief.
He showers, breathing like a fighter, rubs down
And quick-steps to his closet for a suit,
Dark gray, its creases and lapels like knives.
He studies the mirror, not sure of what he sees.

"So, tell me what I want to hear," he says;
He laughs like old-time radio and goes.

CHAPTER FOUR

That life of rocks and rainy wind was good . . .

THE EIGHTIES

Elaine and Tom move on. They live abroad,
As far from Al's designs as possible.
Their only link with home is Eleanor,
Whose letters tell of working overtime
Because she loves the feel of doing it
For no one but herself. Her business thrives,
And just the other day Al spoke to her,
Despairing, as ever, over his son's decline.
He told her how he'd overheard a fool
Declare at lunch that Tom, the bum, had quit
The job to run off with a colored girl.
Al stepped right up, but then was at a loss.

"She's dark because she lies out in the sun,"
Was all he thought to say. The others blinked,
The one who talked made quick work of his food,
Apologized and scrambled up to go.

You both know that's the world, she writes to them.
So many find it easy not to think.

The latest letter moves to lighter ground,
Explaining renovations to the house,
Except for Tom's old room, which will not change.
Tom laughs to think of it, one room the same.

In Gort, beyond a bridge, the sun goes down.
They watch the dogs among the clouds break up
And feel all urgency evaporate.
Inside their cottage Tom lays out a supper
Of fish and soda bread. Elaine leaves off
Her writing for the night and props a chair
Against the door to let the evening in.

The weather soft, the cattle home on time,
They talk about how lucky they have been
To find and work their fifteen acre farm.
Tom's ancestor had fought and fled from there,
And when they visited, they felt at home.

In six months they were back, this time to stay.
Their neighbors taught them what they had to know.
They fit in among people who would smile
While passing you on the road, whose families
Were confident and rooted as the oaks
That cut in their small pasture to the south.

The drive to get ahead, the Yankee hustle,
Was easy to forget.
                        Their slow meal done,
They walk out on a tour. Nearby they stop
To fit a stone up on a pasture wall
And both of them feel part of it—gray slate
And casual motion, water and green, green grass.

The feeling does not last. A year goes by,
Then one day Al's blunt telegram arrives:

Your mother sick. Stop. Big C. Stop. Call at once. Stop.
Come home. Stop. Could use you, sorry. Stop.

Tom lingers on that last apology,
Imagining the jolt in his father's brain
That induced the hand to write it. He clears his mind,
Deciding that Al was panicking again,
His usual state when *sorry* surfaces.
It's then that he thinks of mother doomed in bed,
But he has always thought of his family
As cancer patients waiting to be called.
It hurts to think his mother will be first.

She prays when daily therapy is over.
No mirrors should stalk her in this restful hour;
Her functions peaceful, declining like the moon,
Like one small chunk that flies off on its own.
Instead of soothing walls her room is yellow,
Its color magnified by shining tile.
She sees herself in every square of it
And tries to stamp her mocking shadow out
While stumbling through the bathroom door.
                                                    She falls.

She sees her after-treatment face up close
And covers it with baggy, bony hands
Once beautiful. Appraising the sack she's become,
She parts her hands and vomits on the tile.
Relieved, lightheaded, she folds back on a haunch
And stares into the steaming mass of it,
Of her after the chemicals and prayer—

"My daddy's home again," she softly sings,
"And Momma said one day I'd follow him."

At night, asleep, she's dreaming she's a girl
Whose arm connects with ghosts and runs away.
A small electric clock obstructs the road
Until it falls back on its lethal stem.
But Eleanor can't miss her wake-up call,
A one-armed girl who learns to use her feet.
She has put the weak remaining arm away
And by example teaches everyone
How full a challenged life can really be.
In Dream Land she is famous. Her heart is good.

One day as she is cooking, the rebellious arm
Comes back. It vaults the kitchen floor on its palm
And startles her, then climbs her trouser leg
To reattach itself. The elbow throbs.
Acknowledging the weight of returning arm
She leans a little to one side and moans.
The girl and arm need privacy, some talk.
She wants to show this vagabond the things
She's taught herself to do, so out of spite,
And out of habit, too, she uses her foot
To open the door and window of her study.
Inside she lays the arm along the table,
Its private side exposed, confronting her,
Revealing someone's face in it, related
Yet not her own.
                    "Go on," says Eleanor,
"Explain why you deserted me like that."
The arm replies
                    "I left because of you."
She thinks of squeezing blood out of that face,
But cannot curl the fingers far enough.

"Your tension as you slept exhausted me.
All night you'd thrash and twitch, expecting me
To push away or wave the shadows off.
I flew out after them, then into them,
Until the night I joined them, free of you,
A pinwheel player, a part of many stories
And free to turn a page or close a door
Because my own will called for it. Think back.
Recall us in the Forties, selling bonds?
You chanted slogans; I pumped a stupid sign
And wondered why you did not choose the beach
To take the sun, but hunger overcame
Your politics, thank God, in time for lunch."

"You're making fun of me," says Eleanor.

"It's just to make a point," the arm replies.
"Before I left you never felt enough
Or finished anything you ever started.
Remember Castroville, our welcome there.
I flexed with readiness. My sibling sagged.
Those workers had a laugh. They sized you up
And sent us off to pick; you bent at the waist
And crept along a row of artichokes.
By noon the insides of your thighs were chafed.
You walked out aching with disillusionment."

"Please stop," says Eleanor. Her eyes tear up,
And then the arm comes close to stroke her hair.

"I'm back to stay," the arm tells Eleanor,

And she is whole again, awash in light.

At the hospital Tom fidgets in the lounge.
He mumbles as he reads in magazines
How millions starve and bones break out of skin;
Imagining his mother on that street,
Her joints distorted, the thin flesh of her face
Transparent, her belly a pod about to burst.

—Power Through Strength—Peacekeeper Missile—

The language under the photographs is cold.
Tom wishes he could enter radio,
And that wish leads him back to other days
Of battle, scarring stand-offs, school suspensions;
Because he was the biggest boy in class,
They made him run the washer in the kitchen.
His friends ate in the lunchroom, laughed and left
While he ferried dishracks through great bursts of steam
And daydreamed he was elsewhere, anywhere
Up north, half-mad in the Arctic, exploring ice,
Or in a family like on TV.

Alone Tom tears through glossy photographs,
 Struggling with the tonnage of his country,
The rubbish he climbed out of overseas;
And as he calms himself with Ireland
A doctor comes in with expected news.

Tom sits down in the darkened yellow room
And holds his mother's hand. She fights to rise
As he sings softly, leaning to her ear;
She falls back into sedatives, release.

...Al stares into his spotted shaving mirror
And doubts that he is clean. On last week's drive
From Vegas to L.A. the windows were down.
What secret, lethal test air did he breathe?
On one watch, sweating in the waiting room,
He read about a movie shot out there;
In twenty years the cast and crew were dead.
Al feels some cancer working now in him,
Imagines touching it, reaching down
Into the muck and cold of personal slime
And pulling out a lizard he'd dissected
In Forty-something for a science class.
He dries his fingers on a trouser leg
And thinks of Eleanor, her power plays,
The distancing she stamped into his face,
The beauty that enthralled him when they were young.
He tells the mirror
              "Now Boss, don't drop your guard.
Intimidation saved you more than once.
She'll pull through this. She comes through everything.
You'll be ok. You helped her through this stretch.
She'll owe you plenty after what you've done."

Al puffs up in his clothes, a man in charge
Of anti-cancer boys in his employ,
In his imagination. He knots his tie.
In fact, his suits are looser now than ever.
Death's shrinking has begun, the brisk decline
That punishes and lies, reminding him
For one brief moment of his thinner days.
Al's own face in the mirror becomes his son's;
It mocks him and accuses, spouting lists

Of arms and legs he broke along his climb.
Al mutters "them or me" and shakes his coat
As if his enemies were tucked inside,
Then looks around his bland, expiring room.
He fixes on his dog asleep, so old
In dreams he might be sleeping his master's sleep.

      Tom drives to his motel and locks the door.
He punches out a transatlantic call
Before settling on the bed with an open pint.
Elaine absorbs the news, agrees to come,
And tells him not to smoke or drink too much.
Tom promises. He hangs the receiver up.
With curtains closed, he lies back in the dark
And listens to the distant freeway hum,
Like office chatter roughing up his head.
The bottle moves from mouth to nightstand top.
He works remote control for evening news
And mutes the sound, watching faces move.
Tom turns it up when the President appears,
But bored with doublespeak he turns away
To fan the pages of the bedside Bible.

The Scriptures offer little comfort now,
So a pounding at the door is welcome news.
But when he opens up he turns away
And slouches bedward. He lifts the Book again,
And with a little sneer he tosses it
Across the room. His father bobbles once,
Then gets the Book in hand, then looks confused.
He jams it behind the TV.
                    "A drink?" Tom offers.

Al rips the wrapper from an extra glass
And drains the pint.
                    "I brought another one,"
He says, and makes a fifth of scotch appear.
"I missed you at the hospital," he says.

Tom mutes the President, considers trying
Remote control on Al, but quotes instead:

> *For the idols have spoken vanity, and the*
> *diviners have seen a lie, and have told false dreams.*

"These lines were getting on my nerves tonight,
And then you had to bring your face in here.
It's a wonder I don't put this glass through it.
So, why'd you come? Don't bother fumbling for words.
Could be you want to say we have each other,
We're all that's left, let's put the past away.
But that would be too human, too direct
For you to stomach. Have you wondered who will do
Your feeling for you now that mother's gone?
Don't waste that look on me. I promised her
I'd close her business out, and then we go.
There's nothing decent left in me for you,
Though I am my father's son. And that's my curse."

Beyond the bed, Al squirms and rubs his jowl.
"I sure could use some ice," is all he can say.
Tom points to the sweating bucket and goes on.

"My life got better when Elaine appeared—
You called her that uppity colored girl back then—
So casual she didn't seem to need
A buck or a blessed thing from anyone.

You men, she said, as only a woman used
To handling passes from hard drinkers can.
But an hour later she led me out the door;
We walked around the neighborhood, her streets,
And she made me talk it out all through that night.
You didn't know her father drove a cab,
Put time in on the school board and city council,
That she worked in a house for runaways.
Her race was not your own—that's all that mattered.

"We married in a little church downtown
While you played golf. Mother came alone and wept,
Her first unmournful jag I'd ever seen.
We said goodbye, we flew to Ireland,
And with some money saved we bought a place.
Elaine was just as happy to be going.
The obstacles she faced were breaking her,
And both of us had come to understand:
Intention, good or bad, is meaningless.

"We farmed a little, tried to have a child,
And after months went in for lots of tests.
The result did not surprise me. The trouble was mine.
I left that doctor laughing, thinking of you,
The way you've gone at life so bitterly,
The bullying philosophy you've preached,
The low sperm count you passed on through your genes.
I wept then for Elaine, who wanted kids."

Al lets his glass tip over on the bed,
As empty as the voice he cannot use.
I wanted you to win, he wants to say,
But only *see you later* struggles through.

The burial complete, Elaine and Tom
Stay on to manage Eleanor's concerns.
Tom keeps his mother living in this way
While Elaine flies east to meet the publisher
Who tells her that her book about the poor
Will soar and wake the politicians up.

"A best-seller with a conscience, that's our pitch!"
The agent gushes over gin and borscht.
"The trends are *Me* and *Now*," she says, "But wait.
The media will tire of all that noise
And come back to the social worker thing.
It makes good copy!" The agent chews, then laughs,
But Elaine's look is as potent as a gun.

"I wrote a book. I told the truth in it
The best I could, but let's just cut the crap.
It won't change much, won't lift too many souls
From inner-city streets I know."
                                        The agent
Seems rattled as she signals for their check;
Her time is booked throughout the afternoon,
And Elaine must pack to catch an evening flight.

At Elaine's hotel the elevator coughs
And locks between two floors. A woman squeals
When the light goes out. A man's voice hits high notes.
Elaine gropes in the dark, then grabs an arm
To make it still.
                        "You got a light?" she asks.
A voice, the man's, protests hysterically.

"Calm down!" she shouts. "We have to work the phone."

"Just feel for it," the woman whines. "Don't smoke."

Elaine locates a Bic in the fuss of her purse,
And when the spark ignites the others gasp.
They feel like children in a doctor's room,
Their weeping done, the painless probe put down.
Their ghoulish faces floating between floors
All turn to face the panel by the door.
Elaine is first to act; she dials the phone,
Complains to a voice on the other end of it.
Her thumb relaxes, the lighter spits and dies.
Alone again in the sudden hugging dark,
The prisoners emit a collective groan.
The man sweats heavily, begins to smell;
The sorry woman whimpers as in a dream.

The long day passes, then work in the shaft above
Restores the cabin light. The cable clicks.
The sweat-man in his rumpled business suit
Re-works his tie and smooths his beaten hair.
When they escape the three of them step out
As if they've just come back from a long sea voyage.
Elaine supports the woman as all three
Retreat to restrooms down the polished hall.
The woman splashes water, pokes at her hair.

"Oh, God!" she says, "I've missed another meeting.
Do you think I look ok?"
                              "You look like shit,"
Elaine replies.
                    "You, too," the woman says,
Her voice that of a cornered six-year-old.
Elaine, the mother cat, retracts her claws

And takes a sisterly approach. She says

"I always look the same. There's skill in that.
Our time inside that box should teach you things."
The woman says she'd rather just forget,
And charges off to confront her calendar.
Out in the hall, Elaine walks by the man
Who came apart inside the elevator.
She notices his blush, his downcast eyes,
And smiles in spite of herself. She takes the stairs.

In first class, high above the northern states,
Elaine enjoys champagne and works through notes:

So children of our own, she writes; were out.
We swallowed that and vowed to stay together.
Who knows why opposites can't stay apart?
I only know how much he loves. And me?
I know love's hold on me came gradually
Despite my reticence, despite my life
So far from any life my husband knew.
But places he had been put holes in him;
He knows how fast the light inside goes dark,
Just like the grinding city where we met;
So much disaster crawling up our backs,
So many cradles rocking long-term grief.
He quit his dad, we chose to try a land
His people had come from. I went along.
That life of rocks and rainy wind was good
In ways we seldom named, and we were happy.
Even so, the hook was set in us.
I always knew that one day we'd return,
And when his mother died the time was right.

So, now it is enough to print the book
On how I spent ten years down on my knees
For social programs no one cared about.
It's enough for me to bear it, to see Tom through.
He values me, our sad, dark history.
Such adoration was never aimed at me.

CHAPTER FIVE

The great migrations

circling back . . .

THE NINETIES

Elaine's next book, a thriller, outdoes the first.
The money she receives—embarrassing,
Obscene, though not without some pleasantness.
Tom thinks of that whenever he recalls
The cryptic photograph and sign at work,
Which Al put up above the employees' sink.
The photo showed a woman, pencil thin,
Her old skin sagging, a deflated leather bag.
And in gold letters the photo's caption read:

THIS WOMAN IS AMERICAN,
BUT SHE LOST ALL HER MONEY.
TOO BAD! WATCH YOURSELF.
WORK HARD AND GET SOME MONEY!

Elaine and Tom went out to fetch some money;
Elaine and Tom came back with bucketloads.
Tom thinks how like a nursery rhyme it is.
"What do we want?" Tom asks. Elaine only shrugs.
She reaches for his hand and they lie down.

In time they lounge on pillows on the floor
And watch the wall-size monitor for fun.
On channel one, the dog in Section D
Rolls over, watching *Animals Today*;
In Section Q a child recuperates—
He's drinking liquids, sketching body parts;
In Section Z a dented housewife drinks.

"It has to be immoral, watching this."
Tom tries another channel as he speaks.
The monitor goes gray and buzzes out.

     Al curses The Slump sponging his assets dry
And looks out on his smaller neighborhood.
He thinks of the Lodge, looks forward to a drink.
Some take delight in whittling on him now,
But others see the dying in his face.
To them he's Boss, a harmless inside joke
Who's grateful to be asked to cock his fez
And march behind some local majorettes.
Through El Molino, the City of Industry,
He marches to the brass, on top again;
A man who makes things happen, in a baggy suit,
Appearing to strangers as he never was—
A caring man, so tender toward the poor,
The sick and needy, the workers out of luck.
Al gives a quick salute, but his eyes are dull.
He thinks of Tom, his bitch of a daughter-in-law.
They never call or line up on the street
To watch his squad of moneymakers march.
This sets the subtle sneer on his tightening face.

"Another day, another disaster," he sighs.

     Well how do you do young Willy MacBride,
     Do you mind if I sit here down by your graveside—

Tom wakes up with these lyrics in the room
And tries to shake the nightmare from his head.
He wishes he could wake up once at ease,
Like long ago. The boy in Tom retreats.

Downstairs he empties powder in a glass.
He rubs his chest, imagining angina,
And quickly washes down two beta-blockers.
His mother's portrait stares, though not at him,
Its dark eyes peering into zones so deep
He cannot find some comfort there. He thinks
Of how in life she settled inside herself,
Then settled up with him before its close.
He finds some hope in that. Across the room
He leans by the door to breathe the morning in.
The sun is slowly cutting coastal fog
As late-departing, stubborn autumn birds
Wake up and sluggishly begin to caw.
Then wavy rose-light bundles over rooftops.
Terrific, for a moment, is the calm.

"Today we need an outing," says Elaine,
Who has come down from their bed. "You don't look well.
We'll take the whole day off, the two of us;
Lets tour the new exhibits of the decades."

"A day off at the History Arena?"

"Why not? We'll walk back to our childhoods."

"That's swell," Tom says. "Can we rewrite them, too?"

"Get dressed," she says.
                    Tom follows her advice.

After the video that thoroughly
Explains the pricing and packaging of goods,
After the train museum, the phone displays
And demo cars and trucks on pedestals,
Elaine and Tom decide to walk through seasons
In the Climate Hall. They scuff at maple leaves.

"When I was a boy," Tom says, "the grown-ups said
The seasons would be constant, never changing."

"My part of town just didn't have the time
For talk like that," she says. We took what came
Our way. You holed up in your room with books;
If that's deprived, I'd take a piece of it."

Around a corner a robot hands out coats
In snow puffed out of ventilation shafts.
They climb into a sleigh on hidden tracks.
Outside a moonlit house they pause a while,
Content among the carolers. The horse
Starts up, and soon they thaw out in a park.
They shed their coats. Tom shags a whiffle ball
A motor boy sent up with a plastic bat.
The foliage is breaking, tender renewal,
And men in Hawaiian shirts show off their lawns
While barbecues smoke up the neighborhood.
Some robot kids on bikes patrol the streets
As Tom and Elaine slow down outside a house.
Two children play on swings while mother cooks,
And all are smiling as if they've never thought
About a thing. Tom walks the gravel drive
Toward a familiar scene, a huge garage,
Its rafters cluttered, and wash that billows on
The line out back. Elaine knows when to move,
And tugging on his arm she leads him back.

Not far from home Tom lightly strokes her thigh.
She leans into his chest, and he veers the car
Into a dusty eucalyptus grove.
Outside, the air is thick, medicinal.
Undressing even as they leave the car,
They kiss and lie down in a cloud of health,
But neither can claim that healing enters them.

The 605 is clogged, as are the roads
In Al's uncertain head. He gazes south
And sees the cemetery sign uphill,
Its letters white, gigantic through the smog.
"My Eleanor is dead," he mutters. His hands
Make nursing movements on the steering wheel.
A siren sounds behind him, coming fast
Along the open shoulder of the road.
A muscle in Al's neck begins to ache
As he looks back, so he curses as the cops
And ambulance go hunting for the crash.
Al rubs his sagging chest to ease a cramp
And conjures up his high school coach's face.

"I hated you," Al says, "but I obeyed.
I bought the program. You taught me how to win.
But if you were so smart, how come I'm losing?"

Al doesn't feel much better with windows up.
The tinted band across the windshield top
Distorts the light, making mountains blue,
The unreal blue of backdrops in a movie.
Al wants the scene to shift, the plot to improve,
But he is in a still-life on this drive.

He tilts the rearview mirror to check his face;
His high cheekbones are gone, his eyebrows gray,
His lips go slack and turn a purple hue.

     All day Elaine and Tom drive aimlessly.
They get home late, neglect their messages
And try to sleep, but neither has success.

"I just feel lost," Elaine says. Jerking back
The sheet, she ties her robe and slippers out.
Tom sits up, says
                "Why don't you take a pill?"
Downstairs he finds her in the eating room.
"So talk to me."
              "I'm sick of this," she says.
"We've lost what's human in the work we do,
When we despair we take forgetting pills."

"I know," Tom says. "I face it every time
I walk the halls and see the workers file
Through metal doors to fill those frigid rooms
Of icy chairs, of desks like frozen meat.
I sit at one myself and think one day
Some Boss will risk it all and draft the memo
Proposing that the system be revised
For work at home, for twenty-hour weeks."

"Don't kid yourself," she says. "We're years from that.
I'm all for getting out of here. Will you?"

"But what about the movie and your books?"

"The movie will be bad. My books—who knows?"

"I suppose," Tom smiles, "we'll leave the monitor."

"Let's trash it," Elaine replies. "Let's leave it all."

The thought of shedding what they own is good,
But then Emergency is on the phone.
Tom listens, nods his head, and says ok.
He hangs the phone up quietly and waits.

"It's Al," she says. He nods in her embrace;
She thinks of wrapping one last loose end up.

Al does not feel his own dismantling now,
The nauseous rush of his last cigarette.
His thinking fixes momentarily
On an interior, a lab at night.
A faceless surgeon cuts an animal,
Approaching sickness as one more job of work,
While over the door a sign in neon pink:

It is humane (and easier) to die.

Al's mind is spinning, stopping suddenly
To make out fists above a bleeding man.
The face above the fists, Al's face, is ghoulish
In a loser's light. Its mouth is slurring speech:

Oh when I drink all night I am so happy,
So happy I could work the heavy bag.

The drinking shows in his hair. The image blurs,
Yet other scenes are swift to take its place.

The chainsaw neighbor leans across a fence
To slice Al's yapping dog from snout to tail.
Then women from his hotel afternoons
Appear to probe Al's groin with knives and guns.

"What's left," they laugh, "for any girl to love?"

Then dental drills attack his weakening gums
As a voice declares
                    "You're pushing sixty-two!
You must take better care from here on in!"

A head of close-cropped hair bends over him.
What sex? The She/He is Professional.
Al's chair floats free; it's entering a mobile
Of gaping, toothless North American salmon.
His mind, suspended in that silent school,
Slows down to gulp an exit memory. . .

His son pulls out a flask at the foot of his bed
And fills the doctor's cup. They study him
With pity and disgust. His boy speaks up:

"You're right, of course. It's best to pull the plug.
Before, when there was hope, I thought we'd wait
To see if he'd come back."
                              The doctor shrugs.
"But this is damaging to everyone,
Especially to him. He's not the type
Who'd take to baby food and enemas."

In deeper sleep Al dreams a pedestal
With his bust crowning it. The monitor
Is there to store and broadcast history,

And all is well with resting now. He slips
Into a playback of his patterned life,
Successes and small faces surfacing,
So many whose luck went bad when he appeared.
The neon word *survival* blinks on, then off.
The moonlight billows, ghosting through his room,
Obscuring the family photos on the dresser.

"Please tell me what to say in my report,"
The Dream-Boss pleads, but God is a tightlipped light,
And Eleanor a mute, absorbing presence.
If only he could speak to her, he thinks,
And almost senses communication start,
Then just as quickly feels the line shut down.
So her forgiveness won't be as clear to him
As he would like. The room fills up with faces.
No parent-image soothes or batters him.
The League of Spirit Women calmly waits.

"Don't touch the monitor!" a young Al pleads,
As over the Burden Wall the children go,
Abandoning their bikes beside the road.

A hand has targeted the monitor.
Exotic feathers spiral up a staircase;
A dead phone line fills up with heartfelt talk
In summer days where listening is long,
And Al relaxes in a plush backseat,
Content somehow without air or radio.
The life he made is shrinking in the mirror.
The anonymous driver downshifts, entering earthshift.

The funeral is swift. Tom sits alone,
Observes his father's cronies hurry past
For one last glimpse before they seal the box.
At graveside few turn up to bow their heads.
Released from obligation they retreat
To offices where sentiment is slight,
Where Al is one more desk to be removed,
An office to be cleaned and reassigned.
Tom shakes hands with the few who made the drive,
Then walks Elaine uphill, beneath magnolias
In heavy-scented bloom.
                          "Well, he didn't suffer,"
Tom says. "So like him to hurry even death."

"It hit him just like I did years ago—
A shock, a burden he wasn't ready for."

Tom grins a little recalling his father's face.
"It looked good on him. Don't you agree?
With all that make-up on he dropped some years."

Elaine tells how she comforted her aunt
At her mother's funeral. The woman stood
Inside the church door weeping till Elaine
Came close to her and said
                          "My mom looks good,
So good we ought to take her home with us."
Her aunt stopped crying, thinking what a lark
To see her sister propped up by the stove.
So that was one more hurdle they had cleared.
Beside her Tom can taste the smog but laughs.
Elaine locks up her thoughts and drives the car.

In two weeks Al's affairs are put to rest.
Elaine and Tom pack for a sunrise flight
As if afraid they'll be detained somehow.
While pushing on a pair of hiking boots
Elaine sits down.
                    "What kept us here so long?
The child we never had? The work? The cash?"

"My parents," Tom says. "We slipped into their skins,
An obligation, I guess, but now it's done."

    In Holyhead they check in to a room,
Then walk into the seatown, little changed
In fifteen years. The hills are harder to bear,
Their beauty so intense it wounds the eye,
But the looking cures. The past is far away.

In bed Tom lies awake to watch the moon,
And sees the great migrations circling back,
The children home in lands their elders fled,
Back home among their births and burials.
The town clock strikes the hour. It's nearly dawn.
Tom hears the sheep and cattle in the fields,
The blacksmith strike his anvil, the whisk of brooms
On cobbled streets of slowly rising steam.
We're old but we've forgotten nothing, he thinks.
Asleep, Elaine moves close. He breathes her in.
The ferry for Dun Laoghaire sails at seven.

Miriam Berkley

Robert McDowell's first book of poems, *Quiet Money*, appeared from Holt in 1987. His poems, essays, and fiction are published widely here and abroad, and his revised edition of the classic text, *Sound and Form in Modern Poetry*, is forthcoming by the University of Michigan Press. McDowell is also the editor of *Poetry After Modernism*; and co-translated from Czech, Ota Pavel's short stories, *How I Came to Know Fish*.